New
a visual celebration
Zealand

New
a visual celebration
Zealand

photography by Gareth Eyres
text by Graeme Lay

NH

NEW
HOLLAND

First published in 1999 by New Holland Publishers (NZ) Ltd
Auckland • Sydney • London • Cape Town

www.newhollandpublishers.com

218 Lake Road Northcote Auckland New Zealand
14 Aquatic Drive Frenchs Forest NSW 2086 Australia
86–88 Edgware Road W2 2EA United Kingdom
80 McKenzie Street Cape Town 8001 South Africa

ISBN: 1 877246 22 0

Managing Editor: Renée Lang
Design: Sally Hollis McLeod/Moscow Design
Editor: Diana Harris
Printed by Tien Wah Press (Pte) Ltd

10 9 8 7 6 5 4 3 2

Front cover: Aoraki/Mt Cook, Southern Alps
Back cover: Abel Tasman National Park
Front flap: Rainforest, Oparara, West Coast
Endpapers: Kumara Beach, West Coast
Half-title page: Lake Pukaki, Mackenzie Country
Title page: Mount Ngauruhoe, Tongariro National Park
Contents page: Anapai Bay, Abel Tasman National Park

IN EVERY SENSE **A NEW LAND**

SHAPED BY WATER, ICE AND FIRE

New Zealand is, in every sense of the word, a new land. Once part of an ancient super-continent named Gondwanaland, the fragment which was to become known as New Zealand began to drift away from the landmass between 80 and 110 million years ago, driven by expanding forces deep within the Earth's crust. The land was then submerged for aeons beneath the southern sea before being heaved from the water by more tectonic forces. Its present topography has been shaped during the last 100,000 years – a blink of the eye in geological time.

The geological forces which had separated, submerged and uplifted the land had not ceased their work, however. Proto-New Zealand lay directly across the meeting place of two of the Earth's greatest crustal plates – the Indo-Australian and the Pacific – which drift like gigantic rafts upon the planet's molten interior. Where the two meet the Pacific Plate is continually being drawn beneath the Indo-Australian, creating a zone of geological instability which slashes across the land and continues out beneath the Pacific Ocean. Volcanic explosions cauterised much of the northern part of the new land, while from the time it was raised from the sea climatic forces had also set about altering its morphology.

During New Zealand's geological evolution the climate was inconstant, however. The Ice Ages – freezing glacial periods mixed with warmer eras – ended in New Zealand only about 12,000 years ago, ushering in the current period of warmer climate. Glaciers – moving rivers of ice – from the colder eras left indelible marks on the southern parts of the young land as they spread out and sculpted its valleys into distinctive landforms.

The young land was thus shaped by water, ice, fire, wind and wave into two long islands and many smaller ones, extending 1600 kilometres in its entirety from north to south and rising to

Volcanic activity in the North Island's Tongariro National Park

a maximum height of 3764 metres in the larger South Island and 2997 metres in the North. Located between latitudes 34° and 47° South, and well watered by maritime rain-bearing winds blowing mainly from the south-west, the islands' natural vegetation was broadleaf and podocarp forest, which flourished in all but the drier margins of their eastern regions. The land area totalled 265,000 square kilometres, only a little less than that of Italy or Britain, while its least distant large neighbour, Australia, lay nearly 2000 kilometres away to the north-east. The sea was an almost inescapable presence, no place being further than 150 kilometres from a coast.

The plains, valleys, forests and mountains were the preserve of a variety of birds, two species of bat, three of frog, a small relative of the dinosaurs, some lizards, earthworms, snails and insects. Some of these creatures had lived in Gondwanaland, others had flown or drifted to the islands after the detachment. In the total absence of predators, many of the birds – moa, kiwi, kakapo, takahe – evolved into flightless herbivores, very well adapted to an environment without humans, but much less so when the latter arrived and brought with them predatory rats, cats, ferrets and stoats.

A young land, and one which was also the last to be discovered and settled by human beings. Only in the last millennium, a mere heartbeat in human history, have New Zealand's beaches, plains, valleys and mountains been walked upon by people. All New Zealanders are immigrants, whether they came in double-hulled sailing canoes from tropical Polynesia or in a windjammer from Liverpool. It is the varying times of their arrival and the different cultural luggage which they brought with them that marks them apart from one another.

The first immigrants came from eastern Polynesia, crossing the South Pacific in double-

hulled canoes propelled by sails of woven pandanus, the hulls hewn from rainforest trees. These vessels were capable of carrying 100 men, women and children at a time. Their ancestors had reached the eastern Pacific 1000 years earlier, and had originated in South-east Asia two millennia before that, filtering eastward through the archipelagos of the western Pacific before dispersing throughout the scattered volcanic islands of what today are called the Marquesas, the Society Islands and the Cook Islands. The generic name for the people of these islands was Maori.

The island of departure for these first immigrants to New Zealand may have been Raiatea in the Society Islands, Rarotonga in the Cook Islands or Rapa or Mangareva in the Australs. In the absence of conclusive evidence the exact island will probably never be known, but whichever it was, in Maori legend it remains Hawaiki, the spiritual font of the Polynesian people and the place to which the spirits of their dead return after mortal life has ended.

First arrival and settlement was probably in the far north of the North Island, in about the eleventh century AD. The seafarers found the new land – which they came to call Aotearoa, 'Land of the Long White Cloud' – physically and climatically very different to the volcanic, reef-girded islands they had turned their backs on. The geographic differences obliged them to adopt new methods of hunting, food-gathering, fishing, crop-raising and building.

The first settlers adapted well to conditions in the new, cool, extensive land. They crafted tools and garments from different materials and grew new crops to replace tropical plants such as taro and banana, which could not survive in the temperate southern islands of Aotearoa. They had brought with them rats (kiore) and dogs (kuri), and one crop which did successfully transplant to the new land – at least in the milder north – the kumara or sweet potato. Some time later, the dog died out.

The Polynesian settlers gathered the plentiful shellfish, caught fish with bone hooks and shell lures, dug fern-root from the forests and hunted seals and the flightless bird, the moa. The moa was an excellent source of protein-rich food but eventually was hunted to extinction. Maori terraced and palisaded headlands and the many volcanic cones – which made fine natural fortresses – dug pits in which to store the kumara which they grew, mined obsidian (volcanic glass) from an island in the Bay of Plenty and travelled to the far south to collect greenstone (jade) from the icy rivers there and fashioned it into tools and weapons. Tribal loyalties developed and the mana (prestige) of the tribe was often fiercely defended in warfare. Traditions were transmitted orally through the generations and the edict of tapu – the sacredness of certain objects and customs – was a powerful cultural dictate.

Maori adaptation was so successful than in 500 years the descendants of the first immigrants had settled the new land from its sub-tropical north to the much cooler south and the island cluster to the east of the South Island, called by them *Rekohu*, later named the Chatham Islands. The main northern island they named *Te-Ika-a-Maui* – the Fish of Maui – and the main southern land *Te Wai Pounamu* – the place of greenstone – because it was their source of jade. The third largest island, just to the south of *Te Wai Pounamu*, was named Rakiura – 'Land of Glowing Skies' – a possible reference to the displays of aurora or Southern Lights seen there.

Two-way voyaging between the islands of Aotearoa and Hawaiki probably occurred in the centuries following the initial settlement. Sophisticated celestial navigation and the ability of specialist navigators to interpret wave patterns, bird movements and drifting debris made these long voyages possible. In other respects, however, Maori lived in Aotearoa undisturbed by outside influences for nearly 800 years.

Dutch explorer Abel Tasman made landfall in the north-west of the South Island in 1642 and charted a small section of the coast, but after a skirmish with local Maori he and his crew sailed away north without setting foot on either of the two main islands. It was not until 127 years later, in 1769, that Englishman James Cook, partly in search of Terra Austral Incognita – the mythical Great Southern Land – became the first European to land in the country Tasman had called

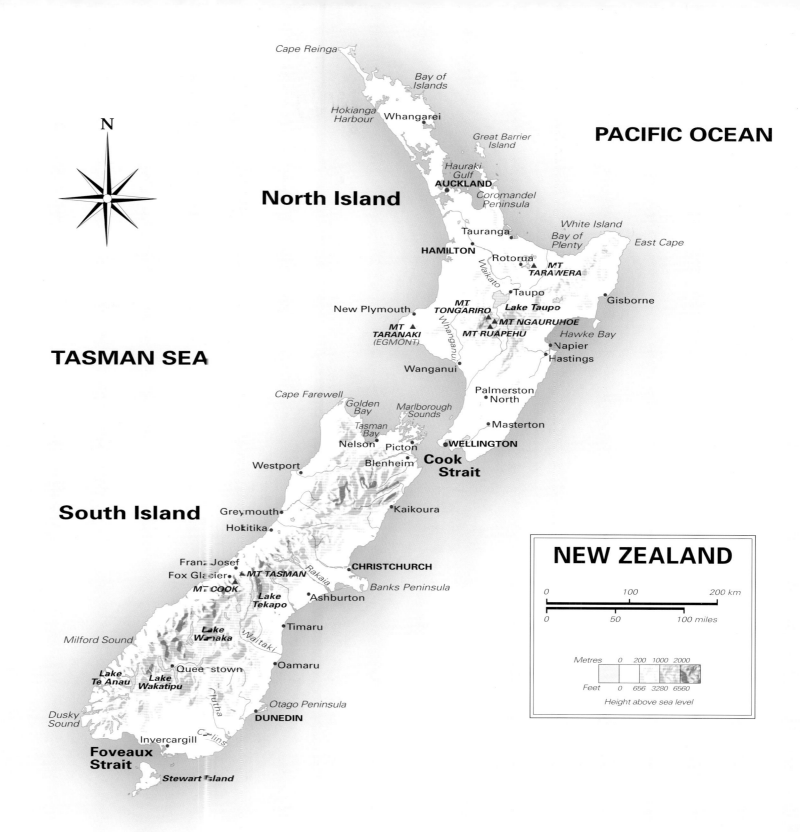

Cape Reinga

Bay of
Islands

PACIFIC OCEAN

Hokianga
Harbour · Whangarei

Great Barrier
Island

North Island

Hauraki
Gulf
AUCKLAND

Coromandel
Peninsula

White Island

· Tauranga

Bay of
Plenty

East Cape

HAMILTON

Rotorua

▲ *MT*
TARAWERA

Waikato

· Taupo

· Gisborne

New Plymouth ·

MT
TONGARIRO

Lake Taupo

MT ▲
TARANAKI
(EGMONT)

▲ ▲ *MT NGAURUHOE*
MT RUAPEHU

Whanganui

Hawke Bay

· Napier
· Hastings

TASMAN SEA

Wanganui ·

Palmerston
· North

Cape Farewell

Golden
Bay

Marlborough
Sounds

· Masterton

Tasman
Bay

Nelson ·

Picton

WELLINGTON

Westport ·

· Blenheim

**Cook
Strait**

South Island

Greymouth ·

· Kaikoura

Hokitika ·

Franz Josef

Rakaia

CHRISTCHURCH

Fox Glacier · ▲ *MT TASMAN*

Banks Peninsula

▲ *MT COOK*

Lake
Tekapo

· Ashburton

Lake
Wanaka

Waitaki

· Timaru

Milford Sound

Clutha

· Oamaru

Lake
Te Anau

Lake
Wakatipu

· Queenstown

Dusky
Sound

Otago Peninsula

DUNEDIN

Invercargill ·

**Foveaux
Strait**

Stewart Island

NEW ZEALAND

| 0 | 100 | 200 km |

| 0 | 50 | 100 miles |

Metres   0   200 1000 2000

Feet   0   656 3280 6560

Height above sea level

Staten Land and a Dutch map-maker later named New Zealand. Cook charted the coasts of the
two main islands in great detail and immediately upon his return to England alerted Europe to
the existence and economic possibilities of the rediscovered islands.

The subsequent colonisation of New Zealand was a rather muddled affair motivated by a
jumble of evangelism, expansionism and capitalism. Missionaries, politicians and traders came
to the new land, and when anarchy threatened due to conflicts of interest and land sharking,
the British Government reluctantly stepped in. On February 6 1840, de facto British rule
became official with the signing of the Treaty of Waitangi between the Crown and many, but by
no means all, Maori chiefs.

Immigration from Europe to New Zealand, previously sporadic and informal, became a tor-
rent as the nineteenth century progressed. Harsh social conditions in the industrial cities of
Britain, combined with an often misleading advertising campaign extolling the virtues of

9

economic and social prospects in New Zealand, encouraged thousands to take the gruelling three-month sea voyage to the new land. Assisted with their passage, the immigrants between 1861 and 1891 totalled 272,990, most of whom came from England, Scotland, Ireland, Wales and Australia.

The newcomers bought land cheaply and set about transforming it into productive pastureland. Their desire for land brought inevitable conflict with Maori, who saw the expansion of European settlement grow to an extent they had never envisaged. Land wars broke out in the 1860s between North Island tribes and the colonial authorities and although an uneasy peace was established by the 1870s, the issue of land ownership and rights remained unresolved. Land confiscated from Maori by the government and sold to settlers after the wars caused particular bitterness.

The land of New Zealand now underwent a transformation greater than anything it had experienced since the Ice Ages. In the South Island, the search for gold led to the disfigurement of Otago's river terraces where traces of the mineral were found. In Canterbury and Marlborough huge sheep 'runs' were established, producing fine wool for export. And in the wetter, milder North Island, the bush was milled ruthlessly or burned, and then sown in grass to support herds of cattle which produced butter, cheese and frozen meat for export to Britain in newly invented refrigerated ships. New Zealand's primary crop became grass, its exports pastoral products – wool, meat, butter and cheese – and all going to its main markets on the far side of the world.

Ports were developed in the rapidly growing towns of Dunedin, Christchurch, Wellington and Auckland, to facilitate these exports, and industries to process the primary products also developed: timber mills, abattoirs, tanneries, dairy factories. By the 1900s the population was growing more from natural increase than immigration. In 1841 the European population had been 5000; in 1891 it was 627,000 and by 1936 1,491,000.

In the face of the European population influx, the Maori population at first declined drastically, from about 100,000 at the time of Cook's first visit to 42,000 by 1896. This reduction had been caused by a combination of imported diseases to which Maori at first had little resistance, and warfare. However the race was resilient and by mid-twentieth century had recovered to its pre-European level, the consequence of improved medical care, high birth rates and revitalised leadership. Intermarriage between the indigenous people and Pakeha – the Maori word for European – had long been common, so that a significant proportion of New Zealanders could claim mixed-race status.

As urbanisation and the pace of urban life quickened, so did the demand for goods and labour. Immigrants from the South Pacific islands with which New Zealand had long had close political relations – Samoa, the Cooks Islands, Niue and Tonga – joined the traditional source of immigrants, Britain, in moving to Auckland, Wellington and other urban areas to take up work, most of it unskilled. In 1961 there were 14,000 Pacific Islanders living in New Zealand. By 1971 there were 43,000, by 1981 it had grown to 94,000 and by 1991, 175,000. The face of New Zealand was changing, at the same time bringing the nation closer to its geographical reality as a South Pacific nation with an important European heritage.

So too was the way of life. The arrival of swift airline connections with the rest of the world and cheaper travel in the 1970s and 80s meant that many New Zealanders were able to visit other parts of the world quickly and relatively cheaply. Always inveterate travellers, they could now travel to North America, Asia and Europe with ease. The numbers doing so increased enormously. And as New Zealanders sampled more diverse ways of life 'overseas', upon their return they demanded more cosmopolitan ways at home.

Above: The pohutukawa, New Zealand's Christmas tree, in flower.

Below: These ponga (silver fern) fronds are also a national icon.

The consequent social changes have had a profound effect on New Zealand's urban life and landscape. There has been a rapid growth in cafés, restaurants, bars and boutiques in towns and cities. There is an appreciation of the place of architecture – modern as well as heritage – in the lives of people. Towns like Wanganui, Hamilton, Napier, Martinborough and Oamaru have restored and improved their colonial-era buildings tastefully and stylishly.

A more varied cuisine and a more sophisticated attitude to dining has developed, combining the freshness of local ingredients with vastly more imaginative methods of presentation. The consumption of beer – the traditional Kiwi alcoholic beverage – has declined as New Zealanders have learned to appreciate the virtues of the grape. Complementing this new awareness has been the rapid growth of the New Zealand wine industry, based on a combination of European grape varieties with local growing conditions and expertise. The best whites and reds from Marlborough, Hawke's Bay and the Wairarapa are now accepted as being as good as anything produced from Old World wineries. New Zealand wine is now exported to more than 50 countries, and food and wine festivals in towns like Blenheim and Martinborough are highlights on their social calendar.

Just as New Zealanders have gone out and seen the world, so too has the world come to New Zealand. Tourism is now one of the country's leading industries, with visitors from Europe, North America, Australia and South-east Asia relishing the different experiences which New Zealand offers them. Undoubtedly the leading attraction for these tourists from crowded industrial countries is a landscape unspoilt by the effects of overpopulation or heavy industry. New Zealand's population of under four million is tiny by world standards, so that there is ample space for all. Its beaches, forests, lakes and mountains are now protected, its national parks and reserves extensive. To stand on a Westland beach or atop the volcanic cone of Tongariro or tramp through Abel Tasman National Park is to be immersed in an environment as pure as it was before human contact.

'Adventure tourism' is well developed in New Zealand to provide for the many visitors who relish the appeal of this clean, pure environment. Kayaking, rafting, sky-diving, bungy-jumping and caving have joined the more traditional methods of enjoying the great outdoors, such as tramping, sailing, mountaineering and skiing.

This book celebrates both the urban and the rural landscapes of the young, vigorous nation which has evolved from its unique beginning. Within the islands of New Zealand and their long coastlines lie landscapes which reflect the natural and human processes still shaping the land. The sea in its infinite variations is ubiquitous, whether in the form of a tidal estuary in

Lake Rotoiti, Nelson Lakes National Park

11

Northland, a white sand cove on Great Barrier Island, a tranquil sound in Fiordland or the storm-tossed waters of Foveaux Strait.

Physical diversity is New Zealand's most remarkable characteristic, however. In the subtropical Far North there are mountainous sand dunes, tidal estuaries, indented harbours, long peninsulas and the remnants of great kauri forests. Auckland and its surrounding region, where one-third of the nation's people now live, lies astride the isthmus which is the North Island's narrowest point, with the Pacific Ocean on its front doorstep and the Tasman Sea at its back and the wildly beautiful west coast beaches and forests only half an hour's drive from the city and the sheltered waters of the Hauraki Gulf within sight of its central business district.

In the central plateau of the North Island, in a zone sweeping across to the Bay of Plenty, is a region of intense volcanic activity which created the country's largest lake, Taupo, four of its most recently active volcanoes, from Ruapehu to White Island, and myriad, spectacular volcanic forms in between – geysers, hot pools, boiling mud and fumeroles.

The East Coast, Hawke's Bay and the Wairarapa are a mixture of crumpled upland still rendered unstable by fractures and faulting and pockets of fertile agricultural lowland, relatively dry as a result of being sheltered from the prevailing south-westerly winds. The small areas of lowland are intensively cultivated, especially the misnamed Poverty Bay, the Heretaunga Plains of Hawke's Bay and the graben (rift valley) of the central Wairarapa, all of which have been subdivided into neat rectangles of horticultural production. These are areas naturally suited to the vine, where viticulture now flourishes, while on the rugged uplands overlooking these basins, the traditional patterns of pastoralism – sheep and cattle raising – remain.

The capital city, Wellington, has been built directly upon the great faultline which bisects both main islands. Earthquakes are common in the area, one of which raised the entire region's coastline by several metres in 1855. The implications of this seismically hazardous location are shrugged off by locals and visitors, who prefer to dwell on the unique, beguiling beauty of the capital city's harbour. Built on the steep hills which enclose Port Nicholson,

Wellington affords grandstand views of itself and the incomparable harbour around which it has grown.

The lighthouse at Cape Reinga

The waters of Cook Strait, which separate the two main islands of New Zealand, are frequently wind-tossed and turbulent, yet much calmer waters are only a few hours away, between the attenuated peninsulas, islands and inlets of the Marlborough Sounds. The northern extension of the South Island – from the Sounds west to Golden Bay – is one of the most diversely beautiful regions of New Zealand. Here the wine-bowl of Marlborough's Wairau Plain and the fruit-bowl of Nelson's Tasman Bay lowlands are within an easy and picturesque drive of Abel Tasman National Park, an area which, like so many of New Zealand's national parks, is almost unchanged from its long era of pre-human contact. Here forested valleys and native birdlife, a sublimely beautiful coastline and pellucid streams provide an environment where every aspect pleases the eye and soul.

The long, mighty sierra of the Southern Alps consists of young 'fold' mountains which occupy two-thirds of the South Island. The alpine chain contains cloud-piercing peaks, powdery snowfields, deep lakes, majestic glaciers, broad 'braided' rivers and valleys which bear the marks of the Ice Age's scouring. Set among the mountains are tourist gemstones such as Queenstown, Arrowtown, Te Anau and Wanaka, from where the pristine grandeur of the Alps can be savoured in comfort and convenience.

East of the Alps are the Canterbury Plains, built up over millions of years from coalescing alluvium brought down from the mountains by rivers like the Rakaia, the Waimakariri and the Rangitata Rivers. To the east of the plains and beside the city of Christchurch is Banks Peninsula, an extinct volcano penetrated deeply by drowned valleys which make the fine harbours of Lyttelton, Pigeon Bay and Akaroa. Further south there are other delights: Dunedin, the Edinburgh of the South, the lonely beauties of the Catlins State Forest Park, the splendour of Fiordland's sounds, and the forest-fringed coasts and peaks of the country's third-largest island, Stewart Island.

This is New Zealand, and this is its visual celebration.

13

SURROUNDED | **BY SEA**
THE QUEEN CITY

Viewed from Devonport, Auckland's maritime North Shore suburb, Auckland city at dusk is ablaze with natural and man-made light (above). The harbour bridge connects the city with the North Shore. Sprawled across the Tamaki Isthmus and blessed with two harbours, the Manukau in the west and the Waitemata, pictured here, in the east, Auckland has always looked to the sea for its business and pleasure.

LOOK TO THE SEA

Yachts and motorboats lie at rest at Westhaven, largest of the city's marinas (right). In the background, splendid in the sunset, the high-rise buildings of the central business district step down towards the waterfront from the Sky Tower.

Princes Wharf, the Sky Tower, Auckland Domain with its imposing War Memorial Museum, the inner Waitemata Harbour and the view across the city to the Manukau Harbour in the distance – the icons of Auckland are evident in this aerial perspective. Recent redevelopment of the central city's waterfront has made the harbour more accessible, and the Viaduct Basin, once home to a commercial fishing fleet, now houses superyachts and America's Cup bases, at right.

17

Behind the neo-classical frontage of the Auckland War Memorial Museum (above)
is housed the world's finest collection of Maori and Pacific Island artefacts.

CITY LIFE SOUTH-PACIFIC STYLE
Members of Auckland's Cook Island community enjoy a gathering of their extended
family (below). Immigrants from the Cook Islands, Samoa, Niue Island and Tonga
over the past 30 years have given the city an increasingly multicultural flavour.

Auckland's waterfront has become the focus of café and restaurant development in recent years, as restaurateurs and diners have come to appreciate that the city's climate makes alfresco dining (above) possible for most of the year.

Sponsored summer concerts in Auckland's Domain are hugely popular. Using the Victorian-era cricket pavilion (below) as a stage, entertainers provide evening diversion for tens of thousands of locals and visitors.

VOLCANIC | **ORIGINS**

AUCKLAND'S FORMER HOTSPOTS

The soft contours of One Tree Hill, or Maungakiekie (left), were terraced by
pre-European Maori to accommodate palisades, dwellings and kumara pits.
One of many extinct volcanic cones on Auckland's Tamaki Isthmus, One Tree Hill
and surrounding Cornwall Park were donated to the people of Auckland by a pioneer
civic leader and benefactor, Sir John Logan Campbell, in 1901. Several other of the
city's volcanic cones, including Mt Eden and Mt Hobson, are also public parks.
Young beef cattle graze the lush pastures of Cornwall Park (below), at the foot of One
Tree Hill. The obelisk at the top of the hill was donated by Sir John Logan Campbell
as a tribute to Maori–Pakeha partnership, but the distinctive Monterey pine after which
the hill was named had to be removed in 2000 due to irreparable damage caused by a
chainsaw-wielding protestor.

On Karekare Beach (previous pages), on Auckland's ruggedly beautiful west coast, two surfcasters begin their journey home at sunset. Swimming, surfing, fishing from the rocky headlands and tramping through the native bush along the coast make Karekare and its neighbouring beaches popular weekend retreats for Aucklanders. At nearby Muriwai (above, left), hundreds of Australasian gannets nest atop a headland and a coastal outcrop during spring and summer, before migrating in the winter to warmer climates in Australia.

On the tamer east coast the slumbering volcanic giant, Rangitoto Island (below), guards the entrance to the Waitemata Harbour. The island's name translates as 'bleeding sky', a reference to its spectacular emergence from the Hauraki Gulf about 600 years ago, when Maori were living on neighbouring Motutapu and other nearby islands. At Kohimarama Beach (above, centre) in Auckland's eastern suburbs, gaff-rigged Optimist yachts are readied for launching from their trailers; and life-savers take to the water (above, right) as if someone's life depends on it.

INTERNATIONAL | **PLAYGROUND**

The waters and islands of the Hauraki Gulf provide exhilarating sailing and sheltered anchorages all year round. At left, yachts in full sail stream out of the Waitemata Harbour, on their way to the shimmering waters of the Hauraki Gulf.

COMPETING FOR THE CUP

An America's Cup racing yacht (above) sharpens its sailing strategies on the Waitemata Harbour in preparation for the 1999–2000 challenge, in which Team New Zealand beat Italy's Prada Challenge, making them the only country other than the USA to successfully defend the trophy. The flagship and symbol of international sailing supremacy, New Zealand's 1995 America's Cup-winning maxi yacht, *Black Magic* (right), reaches down-wind under spinnaker rig on her home waters.

ISLANDS IN | **THE GULF**
SANCTUARIES AND SUBURBAN HIDEAWAYS

On Tiritiri Matangi (above) endangered native birds such as the takahe (below, right)
relish the indigenous forest gradually being replanted on the island.
Life on Waiheke Island (below, left), a haven for Auckland commuters, is now enhanced
with the establishment of a number of vineyards.
Kawau Island (left, below), with its historic Mansion House and exotic fauna and flora,
is a popular boating destination.

DISTANT | **EXISTENCE**
OUT ON THE BARRIER

A self-sufficient lifestyle is almost obligatory for the 1000 inhabitants of Great Barrier Island, 90 km north-east of Auckland. The man on the horse (below) has been collecting seaweed to fertilise his garden. Medlands Beach (left), on the east coast, is typical of the Barrier's unspoiled beaches.

Fast ferries (left, below) bring the island within reach for visitors, making it easier for them to sample the previously remote island's natural attractions.

A LAND | **APART** THE FAR NORTH

The Far North is a place of scattered settlements, pockets of almost pristine forest and an opportunity for rugged individualists to live life the way they want it. Living off the land and making do with very few material possessions is a conscious choice for some locals (right).

Tane Mahuta (left) is the largest and oldest of New Zealand's forest giants, the kauri (*Agathis australis*). Estimated to be 1200 years old, Tane Mahuta stands in the Waipoua Forest, in western Northland, the largest remaining segment of a 13-million-hectare kauri forest, most of which gradually fell to timber milling.

In the depths of the forest a stream (below) makes a cool refuge during Northland's hot, dry summers.

PLACE OF FIRST LANDFALL

Said to be where the Polynesian voyager, Kupe, landed 1000 years ago after his journey from the traditional homeland of Hawaiiki, the long and deeply indented Hokianga Harbour (above) subsequently became a focus of Maori settlement and later, European trading, boat-building and missionary activity.

THE HISTORIC HOKIANGA

The area has many historic churches and the Hokianga district's first mission house (left) survives to this day. A priest poses with a group of first communicants (right).

HISTORY AND | **RECREATION**

HOLIDAY TIME IN THE BAY OF ISLANDS

In Kerikeri, Kemp House, the oldest wooden house in New Zealand
(previous pages, far right), was built from pit-sawn bush timber in 1822.
It was joined 11 years later by its neighbouring building, the Stone Store,
which began its life as a mission storehouse.

A SPARKLING PLAYGROUND

The fretworked coast and sheltered beaches of the Bay of Islands (above) are Northland's best-known holiday destination. The area holds many attractions for children, such as these Maori youngsters (left, above), or for summer vacationers who enjoy taking refreshments on the verandah of the Duke of Marlborough Hotel, Russell (left, below).

LAZY, HAZY DAYS

New Zealanders traditionally take their summer holidays beside the sea, where they can indulge their love of swimming, surfing, boating and fishing. At Whananaki (right, above), campers find tranquillity in a coastal niche, while on the west coast fishers take advantage of the rolling surf on Ninety Mile Beach (right).

Off Matauri Bay (top left), the former Greenpeace vessel *Rainbow Warrior*, attacked by French saboteurs in Auckland Harbour in 1985, now lies on the seabed, a mecca for scuba divers – as are also the translucent waters of the Poor Knights Islands marine reserve (above).

REACHING TO THE WEST

Named by Dutch explorer Abel Tasman in 1643, Cape Maria Van Diemen and
Motuopao Island form the North Island's most western extremity. They are seen
here from Cape Reinga, one of New Zealand's most northerly points.

43

BUSH AND BEACH | **IDYLL** THE COROMANDEL

Only two hours' drive from Auckland, the Coromandel Peninsula's bays, beaches, forest parks and walkways (left and above) provide a perfect antidote to the pressures of city living.

COASTAL DELIGHTS

The Pacific waves roll in strongly along the peninsula's eastern coast, creating white-sand beaches and ideal conditions for body-surfers and board-riders. Many Aucklanders have holiday homes at places such as Kuaotunu Bay (below, centre) and Whangamata (below, right).

LIFE | ON THE FARM
THE FERTILE WAIKATO

Dairy cows thrive on the undulating, lush pastureland of central Waikato (above). A combination of rich, weathered volcanic soil and abundant rainfall creates some of the most productive pastures in the North Island. Small stands of native forest, the original vegetation, stud the landscape.

RURAL ACTIVITIES

Agricultural and pastoral shows, where the rural sector displays its achievements, are significant events on the farmer's calendar. Axemanship (left) is one of the most competitive sports on show. Bloodstock breeding, rural Waikato's most valuable agricultural activity, has replaced dairying in many areas. Horses bred here have won many international races; former Melbourne Cup winner Empire Rose, her foal and trainer display one of the champion mare's trophies (far left).

Multi-coloured hot-air balloons drift over the outskirts of Hamilton, the capital of the Waikato region and New Zealand's largest inland city (above).

Near Ngaruawahia, north of Hamilton, traditional Maori waka, or canoes, ply the waters of the Waikato River (left). The present Maori Queen, Te Arikinui Dame Te Atairangikaahu, is based at nearby Turangawaewae.

SUBTERRANEAN WONDERS

An abseiler descends into a 100-metre-deep pothole at Waitomo, in the King Country (left, above). Glow-worm grottos, stalactites and stalagmites abound in its limestone caves.

EARTH'S | FRAGILE SKIN
THE THERMAL WONDERS OF ROTORUA

At Whakarewarewa thermal area, Rotorua (previous pages), superheated water explodes spectacularly from a vent in the silica-encrusted ground: it is the geyser named Pohutu. The banded colours of two of the most distinctive volcanic cauldrons in the Rotorua region, the Green Pool (top) and the Champagne Pool (above and right), reflect the varying mineral composition of their surroundings. The pools are constantly wreathed in steam created by the meeting of the scalding water and the much cooler air.

THE MIGHT OF MOUNT TARAWERA

On 10 June 1886 Mt Tarawera erupted without warning, hurling millions of tonnes of mud and ash over the surrounding landscape to a depth of 2.5 metres and leaving a massive crater chasm at its heart (above). The eruption buried forever the nearby world-famous Pink and White Terraces and inundated five villages, killing 153 people. The geothermal lake of Wai-o-Tapu (Sacred Water) is one of many thermal attractions in the environs of Rotorua (right).

THE MAORI | **PRESENCE**
MAINTAINING THE CULTURAL HERITAGE

Maori culture thrives in Rotorua, home to the Te Arawa tribe. A number of different experiences of the culture are offered to visitors to the region. A woman dressed in traditional clothing greets visitors to a Maori village (above). She bears a moko (tattoo) on her chin and is wearing a pounamu (jade) pendant.

The traditional challenge to newcomers – the wero – is issued by a Maori warrior, brandishing a carved wooden staff, or taiaha (left).

A young woodcarver (right) practises ancient skills at the Maori Arts and Crafts Institute, Whakarewarewa, where carving and weaving are taught and demonstrated. Ancestors, gods and legends are depicted in carvings, with different tribes displaying their own distinctive styles.

NATURE'S │ **BOUNTY**
FROM ANCIENT REPTILES TO RAINBOW TROUT

Whirinaki Forest Park, east of Lake Taupo, provides a sylvan setting for anglers (far left). The forest contains some of the North Island's finest podocarps and native beech. The rivers of the Volcanic Plateau and Lakes Rotorua and Taupo teem with rainbow trout (left) and brown trout, which were introduced from North America in the 1880s.

The unique tuatara (above) is the only surviving species of Sphenodontida, a very early order of reptile which appeared on Earth about 230 million years ago, at the time when the dinosaurs were evolving. Although the tuatara pictured is in captivity at Rotorua's Rainbow Springs, a major tourist attraction, these reptiles are today found mostly on New Zealand's predator-free offshore islands.

LAKE AND **MOUNTAINS**

TAUPO – THE JEWEL OF THE VOLCANIC PLATEAU

New Zealand's largest lake, Taupo, occupies a vast crater created by a titanic volcanic
eruption in 186 AD. Rivers draining the surrounding plateau filled the lake, which
now forms a magnificent vista enhanced by the volcanoes at its southern extremity:
Tongariro, Ngauruhoe and Ruapehu.

THE ANGLERS' MECCA

Lake Taupo is renowned for its rainbow trout (*Salmo gairdnerii*), which move up its tributary streams and rivers to spawn. More common brown trout (*Salmo trutta*) also feed and grow in lakes and deep river pools.

The Waitahanui, one of the many trout streams that flow into Lake Taupo, offers rich rewards at the point of confluence (above) for the dedicated.

Fly fishers savour the joy of the catch (right).

GOING TO EXTREMES

The central region offers plenty of opportunities for excitement: on the Waikato River a jetboat tests the seething waters below Huka Falls, near Taupo (above). Here the swift-flowing river surges through a granite cleft before plunging over an 11-metre shelf. Rafters can combat the foaming white waters of the Kaituna Cascade, near Rotorua (right, below); and canoeists can take the plunge at Tawhai Falls, on the Volcanic Plateau (left, below).

Huka Lodge, just upstream from the Huka Falls, is one of New Zealand's exclusive country lodges. Guests can fish the Waikato River, which is just a stroll away from their luxury accommodation (right, above).

FIRE AND | **ICE** THE MOUNTAINS REVEALED

An early snowfall has topdressed the symmetrical cone of Mt Ngauruhoe and of Mt Tongariro, in the distance (previous pages). Along with nearby Mt Ruapehu, the three volcanoes comprise Tongariro National Park. Ngauruhoe (above and left) overlooks a landscape ruptured and cratered by volcanic activity.

ON A HUMAN SCALE

Sir Edmund Hillary, first conqueror of Mt Everest, in 1953, is still at home among the mountains of his homeland (right).

A CALL FOR **CONSERVATION**

The growing popularity of the Tongariro National Park in recent years has highlighted the need to maintain a balance between the fragile upland ecosystem and the demands placed on it by human intrusion.

With Mt Ruapehu in the distance, trampers cross the snowgrass-covered saddle between the Tongariro National Park mountains (above). In stark contrast scenic spots, such as this waterfall and pool (left), are often accessible from the Desert Road, as this portion of State Highway 1 is known.

OUTBURST | **IN THE OCEAN**
THE SMOKING VOLCANO OF WHITE ISLAND

White Island (above), named by Captain Cook because it seemed to be permanently covered with a cloud of white steam, is New Zealand's most continuously active cone volcano. Marking the end of the volcanic zone stretching north from Taupo, it is situated 50 kilometres off the Bay of Plenty coast, near the towns of Whakatane and Opotiki.

The crater floor is littered with volcanic rubble and dead wood (right), and the rocks around fumaroles – steam vents – are coated with sulphur crystals (far right).

FIRST | **LIGHT** GISBORNE'S PLACE IN THE SUN

The first light of Earth's newest day breaks over the waters off Wainui Beach, near Gisborne, New Zealand's easternmost city (previous pages).

In the full light of the new day, Wainui Beach (below) displays its natural tranquillity.

LOOKING TO THE LIGHT

An Anglican Maori church (right, above), a lonely bastion of Christianity, standing on an East Coast promontory, is one of the few wooden buildings surviving from the earliest colonial period in New Zealand.

TOLAGA BAY WHARF

Like an amphibious millipede, this East Cape wharf (above) stretches from sandstone cliffs far out into the bay. It was formerly used for the transfer of local agricultural produce to coastal trading vessels.

EASTWOODHILL ARBORETUM

Autumn's palette is coloured by the variegated shades of deciduous trees at Eastwoodhill arboretum (right), near Gisborne.

MT HIKURANGI

The rugged terrain of Mt Hikurangi (overleaf), the highest non-volcanic mountain in the North Island and the first place to receive the rays of the sun each new day, means that farmers rely on surefooted horses rather than motorised transport. Hikurangi is held in deep reverence by Maori. Legend has it that the mountain is the last resting-place of Maui's canoe, the vessel from which he caught the great fish – Te Ika-a-Maui – which became the North Island.

A BAY | **OF ABUNDANCE**

FRUIT AND WINE IN HAWKE'S BAY

A tawny, inclined rock outcrop above Havelock North which local Maori likened to a recumbent giant, Te Mata Peak (above) provides a panoramic view of the Tukituki River valley and Hawke's Bay. The lowland of Hawke's Bay is one of New Zealand's most productive horticultural districts, noted for its orchards, vineyards and quality wines.

GRAPES OF NOTE

The sheltered terrain and dry, sunny climate of Hawke's Bay makes it ideal for grape-growing and wines from this area rank among New Zealand's finest (above and left).

ART DECO ARCHITECTURE

Devastated by an earthquake on 3 February 1931, the city of Napier, the main port for Hawke's Bay, was later completely rebuilt in the art deco style (right).

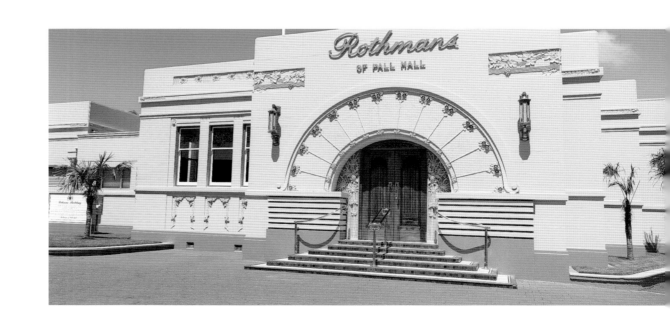

ON THE | **ROCKS**
THE GANNET COLONY OF CAPE KIDNAPPERS

The headland of Cape Kidnappers (above) marks the eastern extremity of Hawke's Bay and is home to the world's largest Australasian gannet (*Morus serrator*) colony. The birds lay their eggs on the rocky headland of the cape (right) from July to October. The chicks fly to Australia at the end of the New Zealand summer, but later return to Cape Kidnappers to breed.

The cape was named by explorer Captain James Cook when one of his party was temporarily captured by local Maori. To the Maori people the curving coastline is Te Matau-a-Maui, the hook with which Maui fished up the North Island.

RIVER | **VILLAGE**
JERUSALEM ON THE WHANGANUI

At Jerusalem, on the upper reaches of the Whanganui River, visitors are welcomed
onto a traditional Maori marae.

Originally meaning the space in front of a chief's house, today a marae is a complex of
buildings, usually incorporating a meeting house and dining room, which has been
built by local Maori people as a gathering place.

The welcoming ceremony begins with a call by one of the older women; after speeches

by the local elders and replies from the visitors, all are invited into the meeting house.
Known as Hiruharama by Maori, the village of Jerusalem was the centre of a Catholic
mission in the 1880s, then in the early 1970s it became a commune settlement led by the
noted New Zealand poet, James K Baxter.

CAPITAL | **SURROUNDS**
A NEW LOOK FOR WELLINGTON

Wellington's harbour (previous pages and above) is enclosed on all sides by steep hills to which cling the houses and offices of New Zealand's capital city. The high-rise buildings of the central business district look across the water to the eastern hills and the distant Rimutaka Range.

Houses in Oriental Bay (right) are typically two or three-storeyed; and like these, have glorious views.

Bold design and construction in the 1990s has renewed the face of
Wellington: on the newly developed waterfront sits the Museum of
New Zealand, Te Papa Tongarewa (above).
A statue of a former prime minister of New Zealand, Peter Fraser,
greets visitors to Old Government Buildings, one of the largest
wooden buildings in the world (below).
North-west of Wellington, surf pounds the rugged rocks of the
Kapiti Coast (overleaf).

PRISTINE | **WATERWAYS**

CLOSE TO NATURE IN THE SOUNDS

A labyrinth of sea-filled valleys, inlets, peninsulas, bays and islands at the north-eastern end of the South Island, the Marlborough Sounds present an unspoilt interface of land, sea and wildlife.

Sea transport supersedes the motorcar, making a jetty far more useful than a garage (below); and canoeists are often kept company by friendly dolphins (above). Passengers on the inter-island ferries are likely to be entertained by the aerial antics of seagulls (left, below). Queen Charlotte Sound (left, above) is home to Allports Island, viewed here from Karaka Point.

GOLDEN | **LOWLANDS** AN ENVIABLE LIFESTYLE

The fertile soils and abundant sunshine of the Nelson-Motueka region support intensive horticulture and produce bountiful crops of hops, grapes, stone and pip fruit (above and far left). New Zealand's first olive orchards were also planted in this area. Nelson is favoured by craftspeople, who appreciate its laid-back atmosphere and the pleasant climate; arts and crafts shops abound, and a rural café near Motueka (left) is a good place to sample the local produce.

A GOLDEN SWEEP OF SAND

Kaiteriteri Beach (overleaf), near Motueka, is the playground of the Golden Bay area; it provides a great setting for a summer holiday.

A SENSE OF **SPACE** NELSON'S GOLDEN BAY

Awaroa Bay (above) is enfolded by headlands at the eastern end of Golden Bay, named for the discovery of gold in the Aorere River – and before that called Murderers Bay by Abel Tasman, who lost four of his men to Maori warriors protecting their shores.

STRETCHING TO INFINITY

The backbone of the South Island tapers away gently to the land's tailbone, Farewell Spit (right), at the tip of Golden Bay. The 26-km-long spit is a wildlife reserve which provides a natural habitat for a variety of migratory wading birds, including oyster-catchers and godwits.

GREEN AND | **GOLD** THE LUSH FORESHORES OF ABEL TASMAN

Named after the seventeenth-century Dutch navigator who came, saw but did not set foot on its land, Abel Tasman National Park and its pristine beaches lie on the route of backpackers tramping through the Golden Bay area (above).

The coast is distinctive for its forested bays rimmed with golden sands that melt into aquamarine waters; ideal for exploring in a Laser-class yacht (left).

Diving, swimming with seals and dolphins and kayaking (right) are other activities popular in the clear waters of the Abel Tasman National Park.

The vast open spaces and varied landscapes of the park attract many visitors, but the absence of commerce or industry anywhere near the area ensure that the environment is completely unspoiled (below).

SUN-DRENCHED | **PLAINS**
NEW ZEALAND'S WINEBOWL

The fertile soil of the lowlands of Marlborough has been washed down from the surrounding hills and mountains by the Wairau River and its several tributaries. The region also enjoys the highest sunshine hours in New Zealand, making it ideal for grape-growing. The land was first planted in grapes in the 1970s and now produces more wine than any other place in the country. Most of the Marlborough wineries are located along the road leading west from Blenheim, the town which is the service centre for the region.

109

MARINE | **WATCH**
ON THE TAIL OF THE WHALES AT KAIKOURA

The snow-capped mountains of Kaikoura, sweeping down to the sea that almost laps at their feet, are a landmark feature of this tiny settlement (above and far left) that has become famous as a vantage-point for watching the sperm whales that pass close by.
The fluke of a whale breaks the surface of the sea off the Kaikoura peninsula (left), while the seals of Kaikoura take their leisure on the rocky shore (below).

ADVENTURE AND | **EXHILARATION** SKIING AT MOUNT HUTT

Nestled in the heart of the Southern Alps, Mount Hutt skifield is only a short, steep drive from the Canterbury Plains, making it one of the South Island's most accessible for skiers. Its high altitude enables it to enjoy the longest snow season in Australasia.

SPOILT FOR CHOICE

From the Volcanic Plateau in the North Island's centre through to the lower reaches of the South Island, skifields abound in New Zealand – making it an attractive winter holiday destination for many visitors.

113

THE BRAIDED RIVER

One of the largest in the South Island, the Rakaia River emerges from its alpine gorge just east of Mount Hutt, pouring out its 'braids' or channels across the Canterbury Plains until it flows into the sea south of Christchurch.

CITY OF **THE PLAINS**
A PROUD ENGLISH HERITAGE

Many things about the city of Christchurch speak of its colonial past such as the Gothic-style Canterbury Provincial Buildings on the banks of the Avon (above, centre) and the Italianate former Chief Post Office in Cathedral Square (right, below). Although it is now a thoroughly modern metropolis, the presence of trams in the central city (far right, above) and punters on the gentle waters of the Avon (above, left) lend a nostalgic air.

THE NEW ALONGSIDE THE OLD

Sipping a cappuccino at one of the many cafés in Oxford Terrace (above), however, is very much a contemporary pleasure.

THE GRANARY OF NEW ZEALAND

Harvest time on the wheatfields near Timaru, South Canterbury. The plains, with their hot dry summers, produce prolific crops of wheat, barley and rye.

MOUNTAIN-FED | **LAKES**
CRISP SNOWY WINTERS

Glistening Tekapo and Pukaki, in the McKenzie Country, occupy glaciated valleys dammed by glacial debris, or moraine. Near the outlet of Lake Tekapo is the Church of the Good Shepherd (right), built in 1935 to commemorate the pioneer land owners of the surrounding region.

CLOUD IN THE SKY

First light on Mt Cook (overleaf), at 3764 metres the highest mountain in New Zealand and centre for alpine climbing and heli-skiing on the Tasman Glacier. Maori call the mountain Aoraki, Cloud in the Sky.

121

FROZEN | **RIVER** THE FOX GLACIER

Thirteen kilometres long, Fox Glacier's surface ice is broken by pressures deep within, originating from the glacier's descent over ridges of hard rock. At its melting point the glacier's pure water is a turquoise shade, a hue caused by 'rock flour' carried along in the ice (left).

The massive dimensions of the ice-flow dwarf a helicopter (above), hovering like a small dragonfly over the fractured ice of the glacier.

THE WILD | **WET COAST** RAINFOREST ON THE WEST COAST

South Westland rainforest has a primeval appearance (above). The main species of native trees in this region include rimu, kahikatea and koromiko, while ferns and swamp grasses proliferate on the saturated floor of the forest (below).

A combination of exceptionally high rainfall (between 3000 and 6000 millimetres annually), mild temperatures and alluvial soils on the West Coast produce luxuriant forest growth.

SHAPED | **BY THE SEA** AND A MINING HERITAGE

The contorted limbs of forest trees accumulate as driftwood sculpture on Gillespies Beach, south Westland (above).

Used houses (right, above) are plentiful and cheap on the West Coast – for those unconcerned with appearance – because the many coalmine closures over the years caused hundreds of miners to leave.

A sanctuary for backpackers, the droll, laid-back Formerly the Blackball Hilton (right) provides economical accommodation and refreshments. The hotel dates from the last days of the goldmining era, in the early 1900s. Blackball was formerly a coal as well as goldmining town, located on a plateau above the Grey Valley, inland from Greymouth, the West Coast's largest town.

ALPINE | **HEIGHTS** AND AQUATIC DELIGHTS

Lake Wanaka (below), in Central Otago, with its hot dry summers and sheltered waters is a popular camping area, while in winter it becomes a base for visitors to the Cardrona skifield.

One of aviation buff Sir Tim Wallace's vintage planes displays its variegated livery when flying over Lake Wanaka (right). The popular biennial 'Warbirds Over Wanaka' airshow is held at Easter.

THRILLS AND SPILLS

Queenstown and the surrounding region offer an incredible range of extreme sports, all of which attract huge numbers of visitors throughout the year.

An inflatable raft enters a stretch of rapids on the Shotover River, north of Queenstown; in turbulent white water it becomes a temporary submersible (below).

'BACK SOON, WE HOPE!'

A bungy exponent takes a great leap downward from a platform above a gorge near Queenstown (right). The Skippers Canyon Bridge and the Kawarau Suspension Bridge are the most popular locations for this heart-stopping sport.

REACH FOR THE | **SKY** A TOP SETTING

Viewed from Treble Cone skifield, Lake Wanaka appears a mere pond, miniaturised by row upon row of snow-clad peaks. The ski season here begins in June and extends through to at least September. The field has runs to suit skiers of all levels of ability.

OPEN FOR BUSINESS

The venerable watering-hole, the Cardrona Hotel (right) in the Cardrona Valley, south of Wanaka, was built during the goldrush in 1868. It deteriorated throughout the twentieth century but has been recently renovated, serving the skiers and trampers who frequent the area.

THE JEWEL | **ON THE LAKE** QUEENSTOWN CHIC

One of New Zealand's most developed and popular resorts, Queenstown makes a superb base from which to explore the many outdoor attractions of its surrounding district.

Like a colony of coloured fireflies, the buildings of Queenstown glow brightly in their sheltered corner of Lake Wakatipu (above). The café culture (left, above) flourishes here, along with enough boutiques, restaurants, nightclubs and hotels to keep the most seasoned traveller happy.

The stately steamer TSS *Earnslaw* (left, below) began service in 1912, serving run-holders who farmed around Lake Wakatipu. Today it takes visitors for cruises on the lake from its home port of Queenstown.

LANDSCAPED │ **BY RIVERS**
GOLDEN DREAMS

Drenched in late afternoon autumn light, the tiny settlement of Macetown (left), on the Arrow River, epitomises the golden past of Central Otago. The beauty and tranquillity of its setting make it an ideal hiking and camping area.

A RIVER OF GOLD

A relic of the nineteenth-century rush for riches, this abandoned gold miner's hut (left, below) once gave shelter to the men who sought the precious metal in the nearby swift-flowing Kawarau River during the 1860s.

The Kawarau (below) flows on into Lake Wakatipu at Frankton Arm, east of Queenstown.

THE SCOTTISH | **SOUTH** DUNEDIN SHOWS ITS TRUE COLOURS

Founded by settlers from Scotland, the city of Dunedin enjoyed subsequent prosperity as a result of gold, which was first discovered in the province in 1861. The University of Otago buildings (below) display the solid confidence of the Victorian era. The university, founded in 1869, is the oldest in New Zealand, reflecting the nineteenth-century importance of Dunedin, then the country's commercial and cultural capital.

THE NATIONAL SPORT

A renaissance in southern rugby in recent years has brought large crowds of Otago supporters to the province's rugby headquarters: at Carisbrook the All Blacks play England (above, left); while on the open terraces young Otago Highlanders' supporters, or 'scarfies', flaunt their team's blue and gold colours at a game against their traditional Canterbury foes (above, right).

A night rugby game illuminates Carisbrook (right), known as 'The House of Pain' for visiting teams because of the amazing fervour and commitment to winning shown by Otago teams.

NATURE'S **SANCTUARY** <small>ON THE SOUTHERN COAST</small>

THE CATLINS

A chunk of hill country which comprises the most southerly region of the South Island, the Catlins is a state forest park containing rainforests, lakes, waterfalls, cliffs, caves and embayed beaches such as Tautuku Bay (below).

BIRDWATCHERS' HEAVEN

The deeply indented Otago Peninsula (far right) extends north-east from Dunedin and provides a sanctuary for penguins – including the rare yellow-eyed penguin or hoiho, fur seals, white-faced heron (right) and the mighty and majestic Royal Albatross.

INLAND **TRANQUILLITY**
THE FACE OF CENTRAL OTAGO

Willow-fringed rivers, floodplains, shingle river terraces and distant hills typify inland Otago. Its distance from the sea gives central Otago a 'continental' climate – the hottest, driest summers and coldest, driest winters in New Zealand. Stone fruit thrive in this climate, however, and the region's developing wineries are the most southerly in the country.

PEOPLED BY MEMORIES

The Vulcan Hotel, St Bathans, on a small inland Otago backroad, is one of the few buildings remaining from prospecting days (left). The discovery of gold in nearby Dunstan Creek in 1862 created a boom town in the following period, but when the gold ran out St Bathans was left a ghost town.

Ruthless sluicing for gold during the nineteenth century created a huge hole in the St Bathans Range, which subsequently filled with water and today provides a recreation area, Blue Lake, for picnickers, swimmers and waterskiers (below).

A DROWNED AND **SATURATED LAND** REMOTE FIORDLAND

Sunset on Mitre Peak and Milford Sound, Fiordland. The peak, aptly named after a bishop's head-dress, is perfectly mirrored in the waters of the sound, the most northerly of the region's 15 fiords.

SCULPTED BY GLACIERS

Fiordland is New Zealand's most remote region, and its wettest. Milford Sound receives an average of 7274 mm of rain a year. The fiords penetrate the land deeply from the Tasman Sea. Around 15,000 years ago, during one of the ice ages, huge glaciers filled the valleys, scouring them out into sheer-sided U-shapes. These deep valleys were flooded by the sea when the ice age ended, creating a complex series of fiords.

A WALK ON THE | **WILD SIDE** THE MILFORD TRACK

The Milford Track is considered one of New Zealand's finest wilderness walks. The 54-km track, which begins at the head of Lake Te Anau and ends at Milford Sound, takes about four days to traverse. Accommodation is provided in comfortable huts along the route.

NATURE FACE TO FACE

A kea (*Nestor notabilis*), a fun-loving member of the parrot family which inhabits the cool high country of the South Island, enjoys a rain shower (right).

The McKay Falls near Milford (far right), like many others in the region, are the result of Fiordland's heavy precipitation and steep slopes. The high rainfall also nourishes dense undergrowth and rainforest on the lower slopes of the land (above).

STAIRWAY TO | **HEAVEN** THE ROUTEBURN TRACK

The magnificent Routeburn alpine track was used first by Maori, crossing from Lake Wakatipu to the West Coast in search of the beautiful pounamu or jade, then by the Europeans seeking their precious metal, gold. Now people walk it to admire the panoramic views of the Southern Alps and the beech forests and alpine herb fields along the way (previous pages and above, left).

EN ROUTE

The 32-km walk takes from two to three days to complete. Along the way trampers can pause to admire glacial lakes (right, above), the bush line and mountain vistas (right, below).

REMOTE AND | **SELDOM SEEN** FIORDLAND'S SOUTH-WESTERN COAST

The land plummets from the mountains to the sea; the further south one goes, the more isolated and inaccessible Fiordland's sounds become, except to trampers on the mountain heights above or the occasional intrepid travellers who brave their icy waters. Te Waewae Bay (left, above), a large bight in the southern coast of the South Island, marks the eastern margin of Fiordland and the beginning of the Southland region.

DUSKY SOUND

In 1769 and 1772 Captain James Cook anchored his ships in the deep, sheltered waters of Dusky Sound (overleaf) during expeditions to chart the Fiordland coast. Sealing ships from New South Wales began landing gangs along the Fiordland coast in the 1790s, to hunt the prized skin of the southern fur seal. Today, seal colonies flourish on the coast and bottlenose dolphins can often be seen. Various vessels take visitors on environmentally considerate trips deep into the sounds to observe the marine life.

ACKNOWLEDGEMENTS

I would like to thank everyone who assisted in making this collection of images possible. They are too many to mention here, but a special thanks to members of the New Zealand Tourism Board who have helped along the way; Robyn Langwell of *North & South* magazine; Imageworks Auckland for their care in processing; Tony and July Monk of Heletranz for the steady flying; Jesse, Simon and Budgie for being the best crew in the country; and to Kate who puts up with all the chaos.

This is for my Mum who never got to go to all the places I've been. If it wasn't for her …

PHOTOGRAPHIC CREDITS

All photographs © Gareth Eyres/Exposure with the exception of the following:
David Wall: pp 44–45 (bottom left, bottom right), pp 116–117, pp 140–141,
p 143 (top left and top right).
Gray Clapham: pp 74–75, 76–77.
Rob Suisted: p 92 (top and bottom), p 93 (below), p 96 (top).

Gareth Eyres is the principal of Exposure, an image resource
of New Zealand and Pacific transparencies.
Visit Exposure's website at www.exposure.co.nz

Hanimex NZ Limited, distributors of Fujifilm, are proud to have supplied
the Fuji Professional film used by Gareth Eyres to create this book.
Fujichrome Velvia and Fujichrome Provia were used.